Disney
Songs for Accordion

Disney characters and artwork © Disney Enterprises, Inc.

ISBN 978-1-4950-5025-1

WALT DISNEY MUSIC COMPANY
WONDERLAND MUSIC COMPANY, INC

DISTRIBUTED BY

HAL•LEONARD®
CORPORATION

7777 W. BLUEMOUND RD. P.O. BOX 13819 MILWAUKEE, WI 53213

In Australia Contact:
Hal Leonard Australia Pty. Ltd.
4 Lentara Court
Cheltenham, Victoria, 3192 Australia
Email: ausadmin@halleonard.com.au

Visit Hal Leonard Online at
www.halleonard.com

BE OUR GUEST
from Walt Disney's BEAUTY AND THE BEAST

Music by ALAN MENKEN
Lyrics by HOWARD ASHMAN

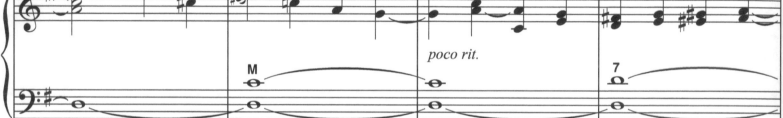

we pro - vide the rest. Soup *du jour!* Hot *hors d'oeuvres!* Why, we
na - ry ca - ba - ret! You're a - lone and you're scared but the
here, and we're ob - sessed. With your meal, with your ease, yes, in -

To Coda ⊕

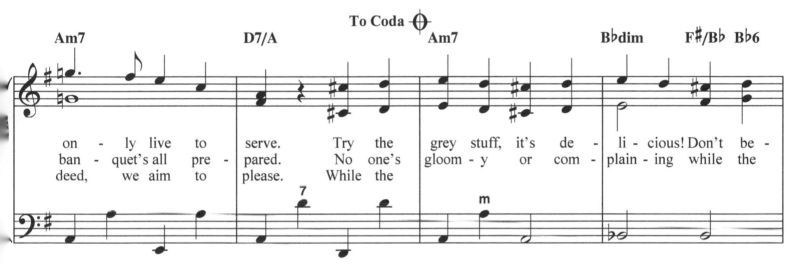

on - ly live to serve. Try the grey stuff, it's de - li - cious! Don't be -
ban - quet's all pre - pared. No one's gloom - y or com - plain - ing while the
deed, we aim to please. While the

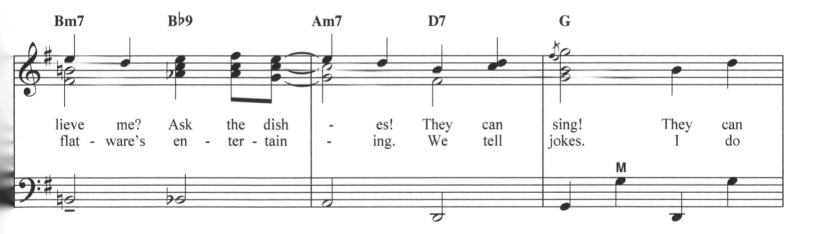

lieve me? Ask the dish - es! They can sing! They can
flat - ware's en - ter - tain - ing. We tell jokes. I do

dance! Af - ter all, miss, this is France! And a
tricks with my fel - low can - dle - sticks, *Mugs:* And it's

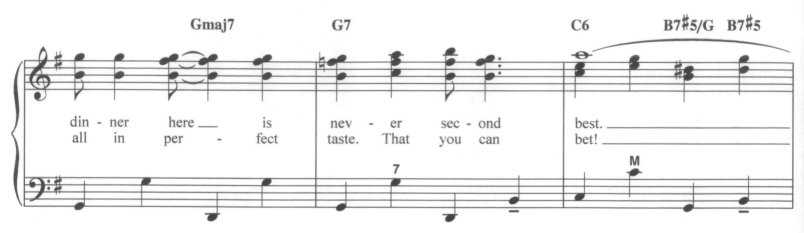

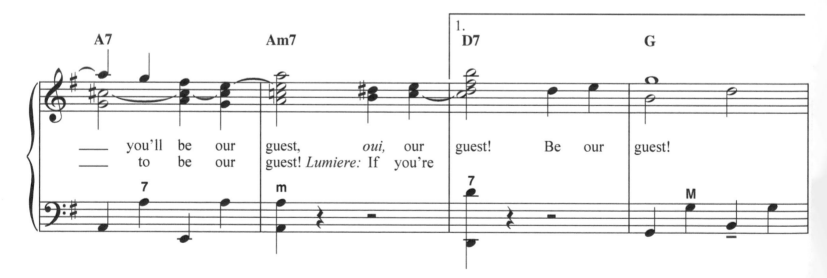

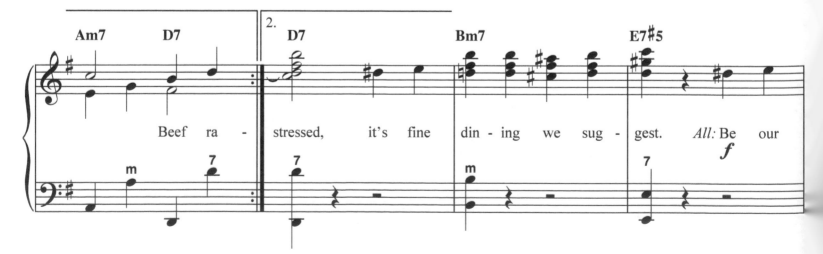

guest! Be our guest! Be our guest!

Slower, melancholy

Lumiere:
Life is so un - nerv - ing for a ser - vant who's not
years ___ we've been rust - ing, need - ing so much more than

mp freely

serv - ing. He's not whole with - out a soul to wait up - on. ___
dust - ing. Need-ing ex - er - cise, a chance to use our skills. ___

dim

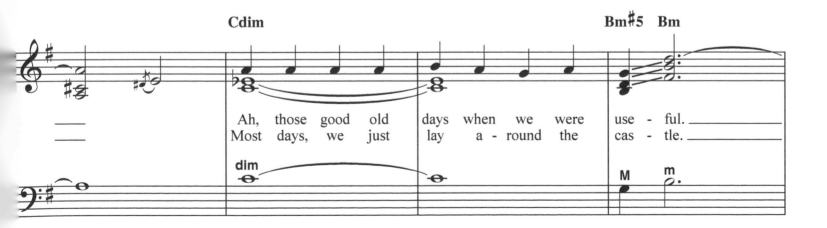

___ Ah, those good old days when we were use - ful. ___
___ Most days, we just lay a - round the cas - tle. ___

dim

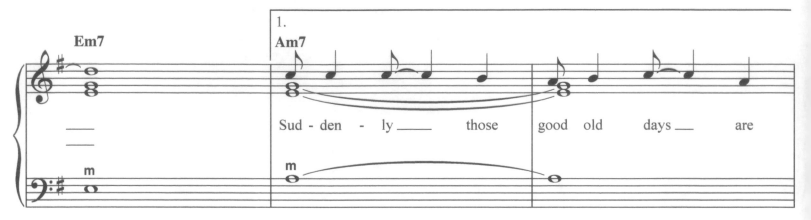

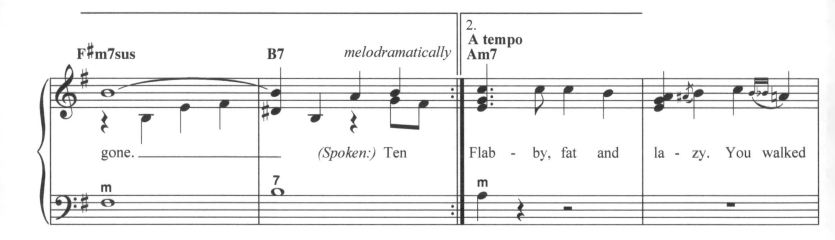

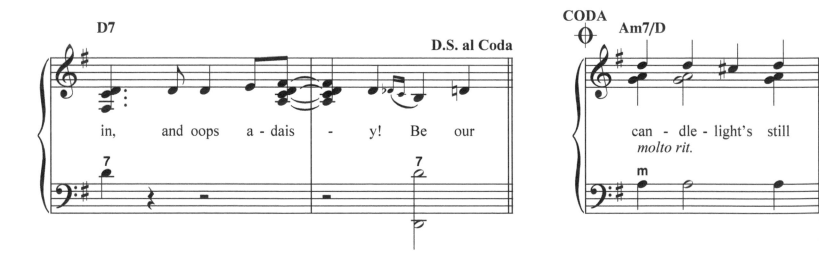

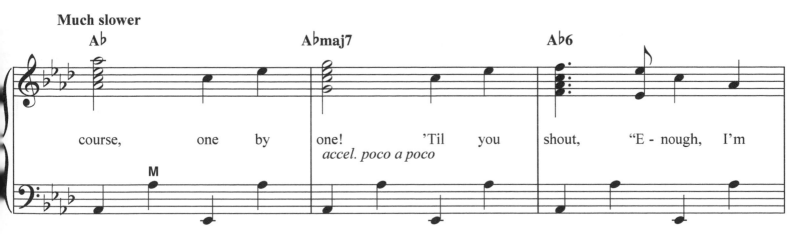

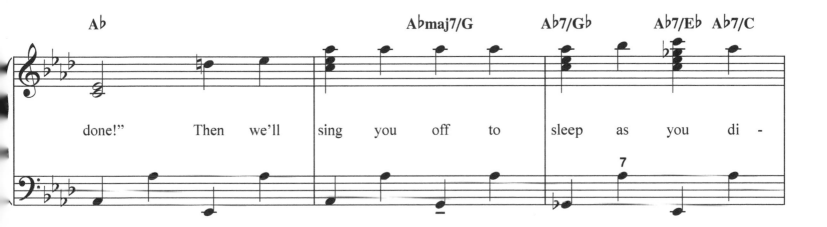

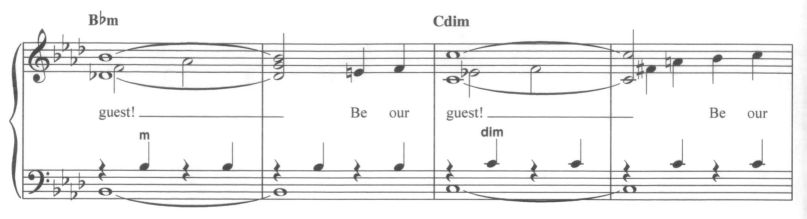

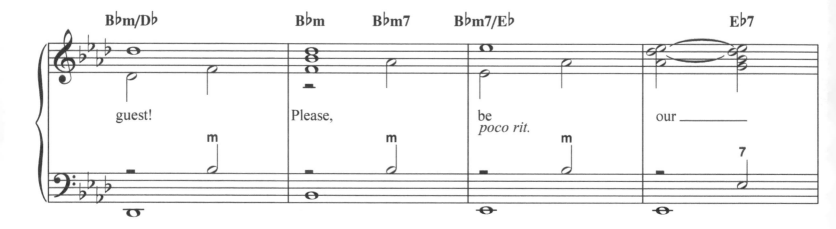

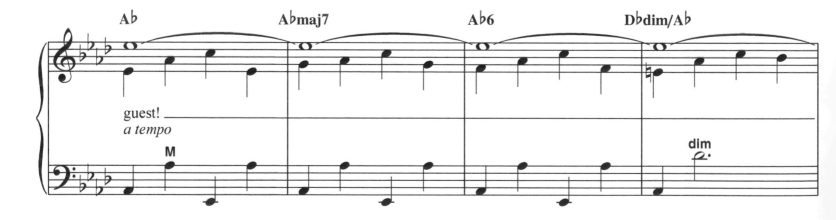

BEAUTY AND THE BEAST
from Walt Disney's BEAUTY AND THE BEAST

Music by ALAN MENKEN
Lyrics by HOWARD ASHMAN

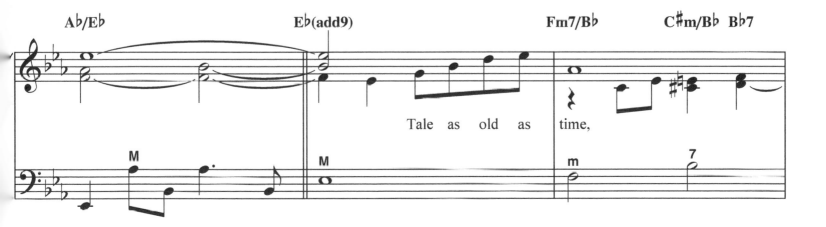

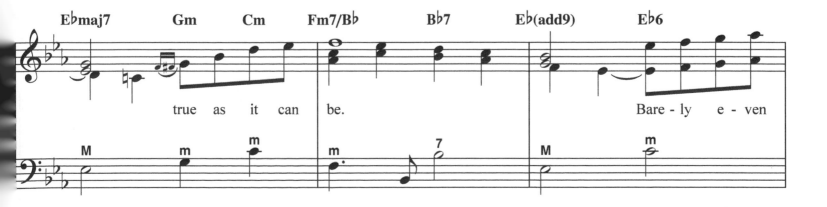

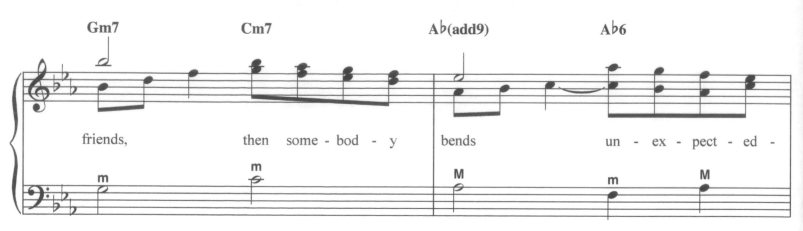

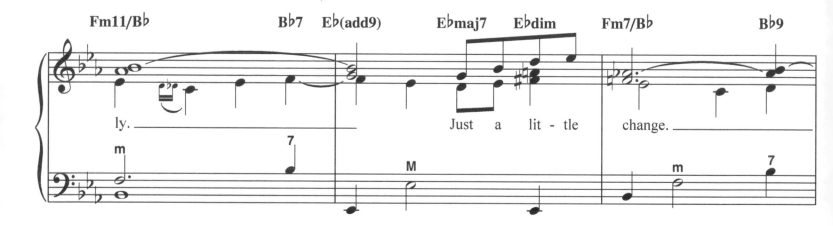

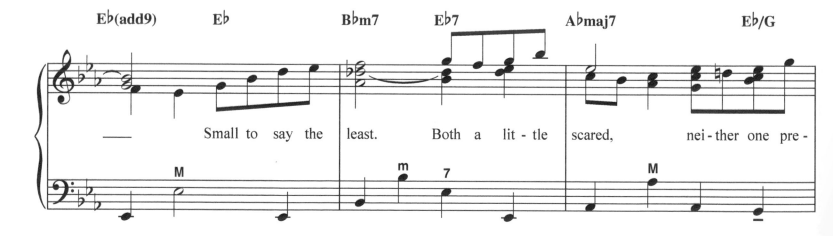

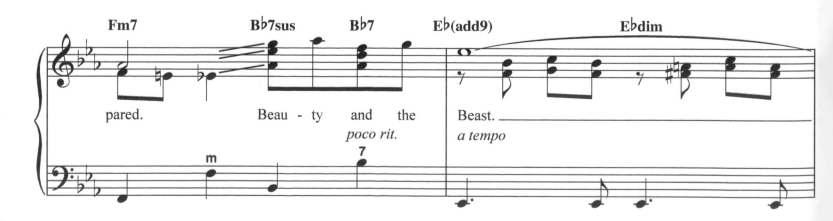

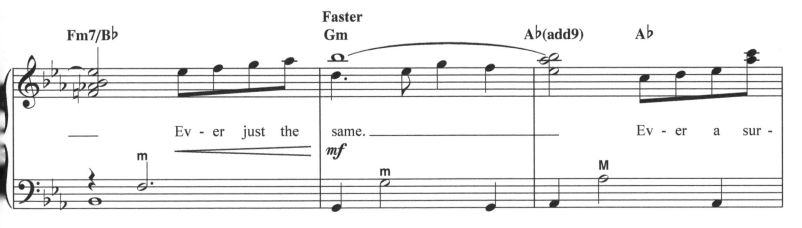

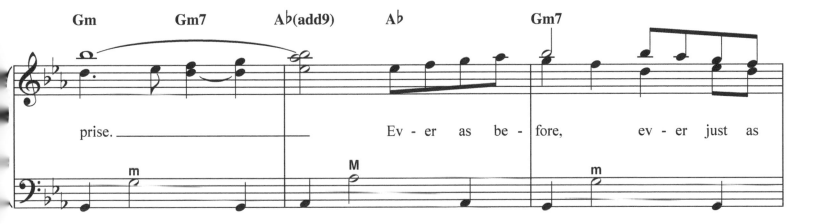

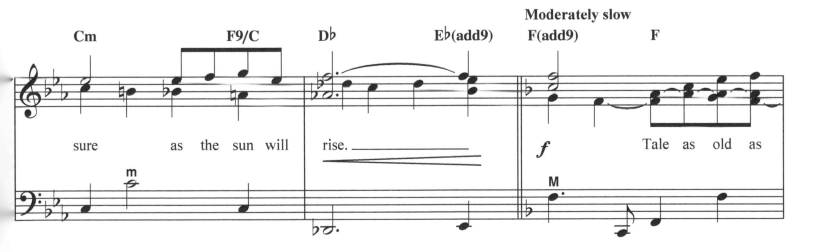

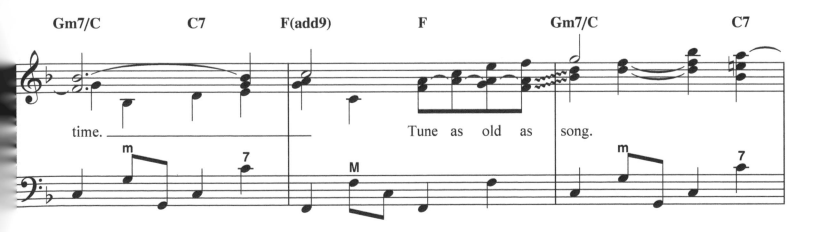

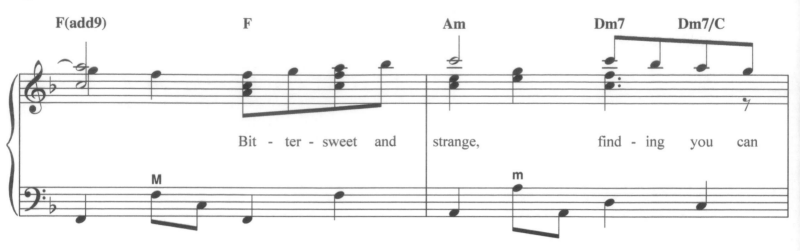

Bit - ter - sweet and strange, find - ing you can

change, learn - ing you were wrong. _____ Cer - tain as the

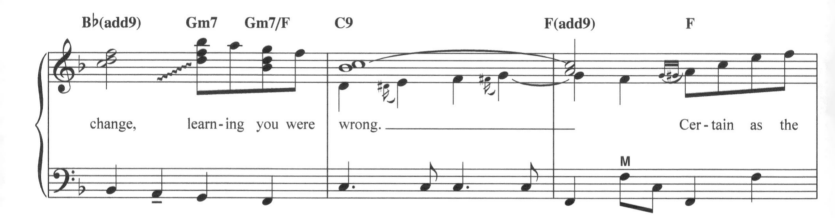

sun _____ ris - ing in the

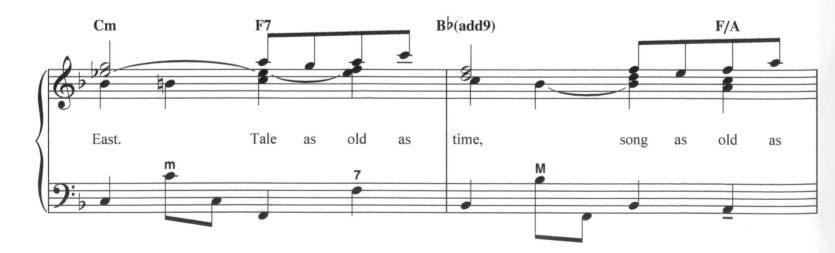

East. Tale as old as time, song as old as

rhyme. Beau - ty and the Beast. m Tale as old as

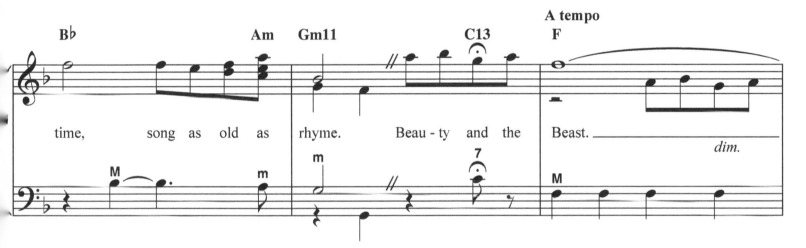

time, song as old as rhyme. Beau - ty and the Beast.

BELLA NOTTE
(This Is the Night)
from Walt Disney's LADY AND THE TRAMP

Words and Music by PEGGY LEE
and SONNY BURKE

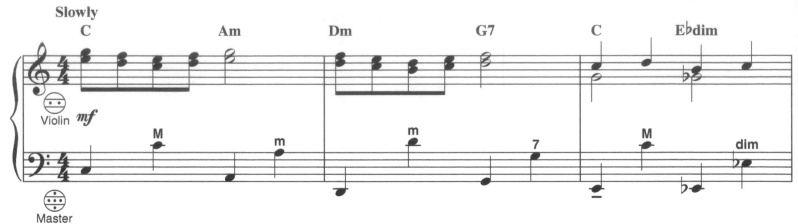

This ___ is the night, ___ it's a beau - ti - ful night ___ and we

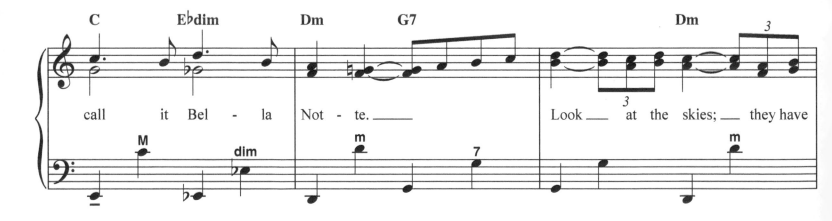

call it Bel - la Not - te. ___ Look ___ at the skies; ___ they have

stars ___ in their eyes ___ on this love - ly Bel - la Not - te. So

take the love ___ of your loved one. You'll need it a - bout this

time to keep from fall - ing like a star when you

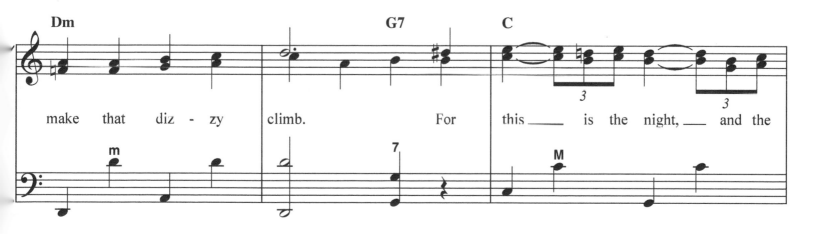

make that diz - zy climb. For this ___ is the night, ___ and the

heav - ens are right ___ on this love - ly Bel - la Not - te.

BIBBIDI-BOBBIDI-BOO
(The Magic Song)
from Walt Disney's CINDERELLA

Words by JERRY LIVINGSTON
Music by MACK DAVID and AL HOFFMAN

Sa - la - ga - doo - la men - chic - ka boo - la

bib - bi - di - bob - bi - di - boo. Put 'em to - geth - er and what have you got?

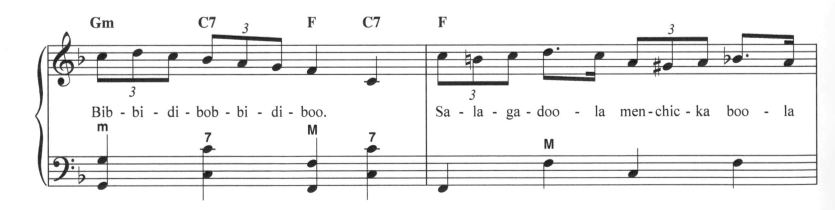

Bib - bi - di - bob - bi - di - boo. Sa - la - ga - doo - la men - chic - ka boo - la

bib - bi - di - bob - bi - di - boo. It - 'll do mag - ic, be - lieve it or not,

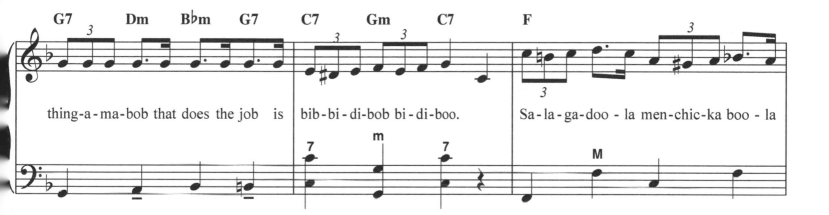

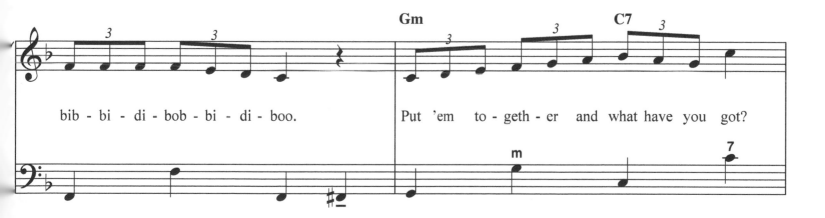

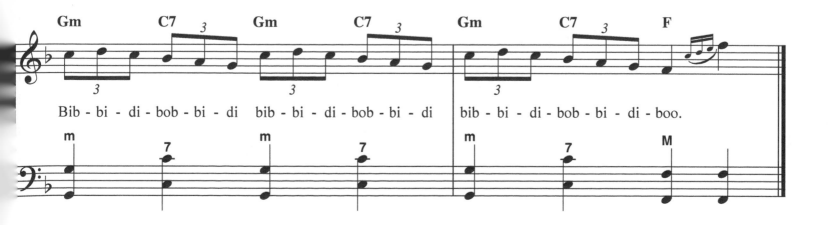

CAN YOU FEEL THE LOVE TONIGHT

from Walt Disney Pictures' THE LION KING

Music by ELTON JOHN
Lyrics by TIM RICE

can you feel the love to - night? It is where we

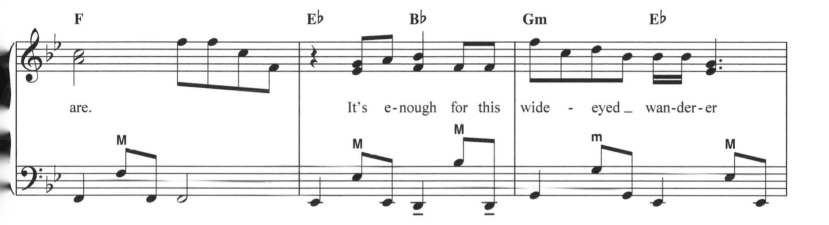

are. It's e-nough for this wide - eyed_ wan-der-er

that we got this far. And can you feel the

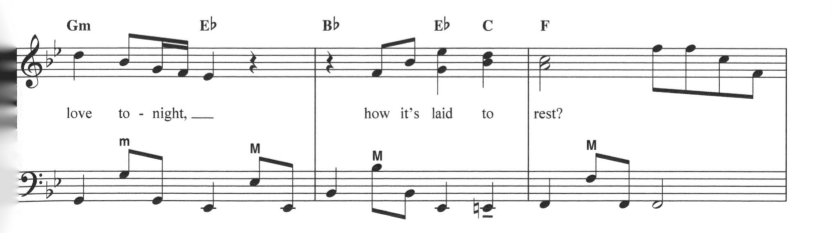

love to - night, ___ how it's laid to rest?

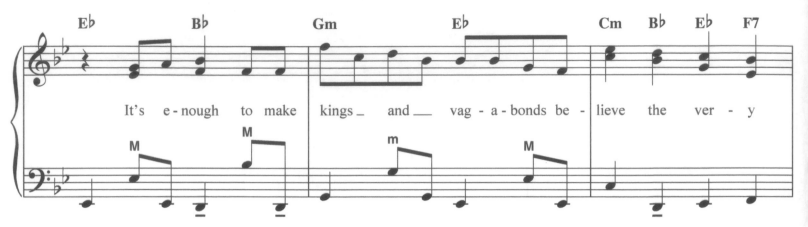

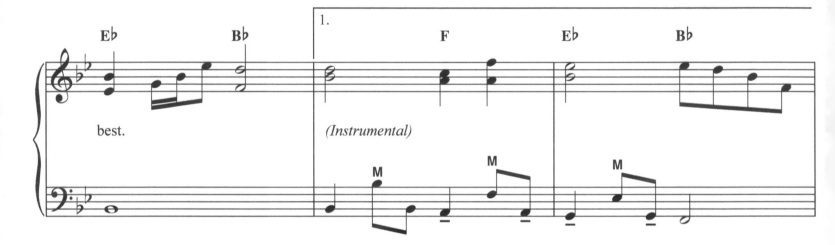

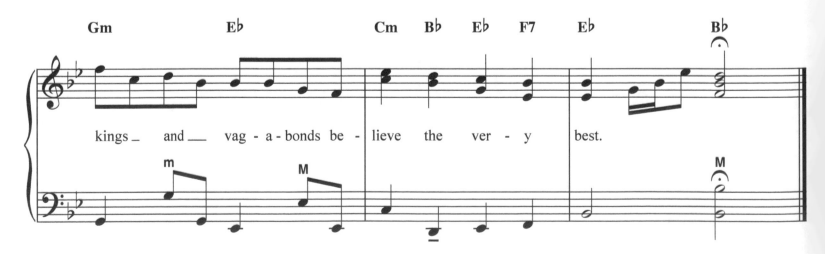

A DREAM IS A WISH YOUR HEART MAKES
from Walt Disney's CINDERELLA

Words and Music by MACK DAVID,
AL HOFFMAN and JERRY LIVINGSTON

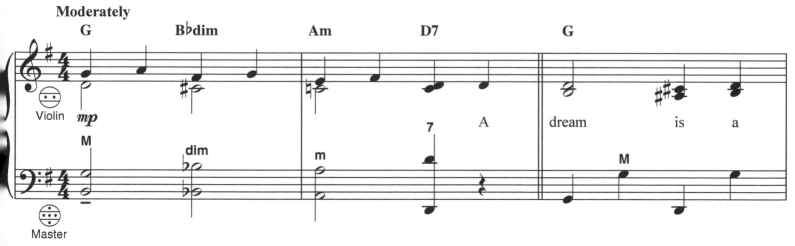

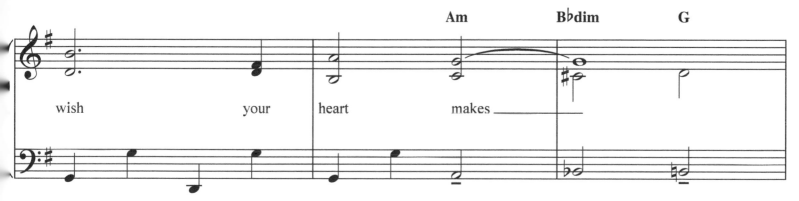

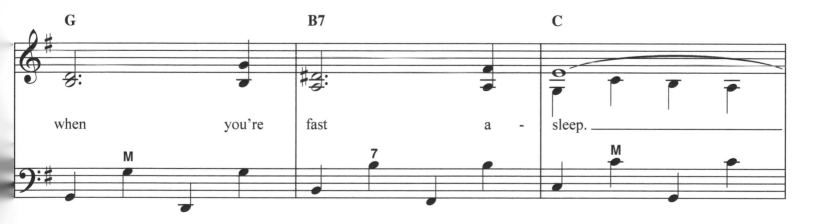

Lyrics: A dream is a wish your heart makes when you're fast asleep. In dreams you will lose your

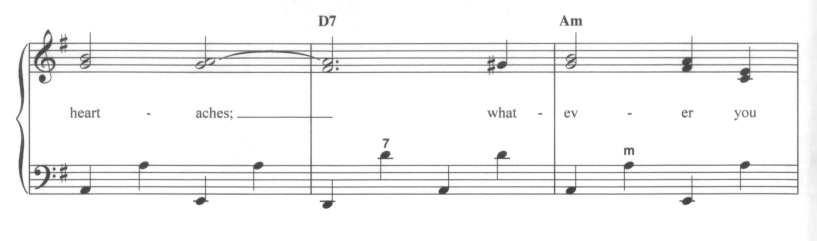

heart - aches; _____ what - ev - er you

wish for you keep. _____ Have

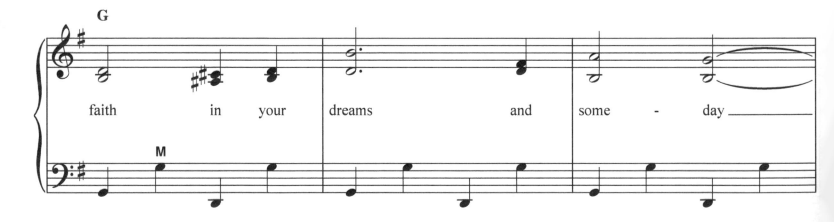

faith in your dreams and some - day _____

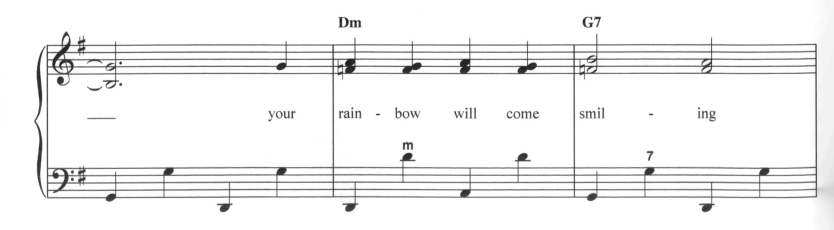

_____ your rain - bow will come smil - ing

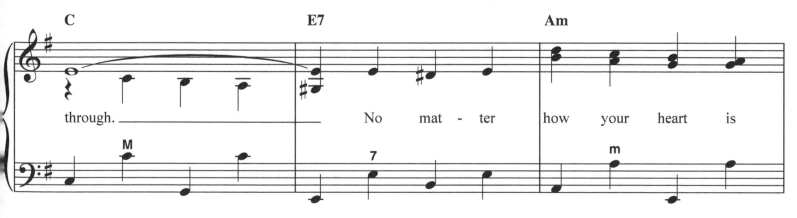

through. _____ No mat - ter how your heart is

griev - ing, if you keep on be - liev - ing, the

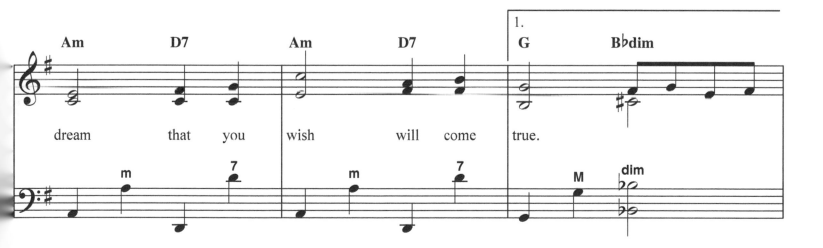

dream that you wish will come true.

true.

CHIM CHIM CHER-EE

from Walt Disney's MARY POPPINS

Words and Music by RICHARD M. SHERMAN
and ROBERT B. SHERMAN

Lightly, with gusto (Play an octave higher throughout)

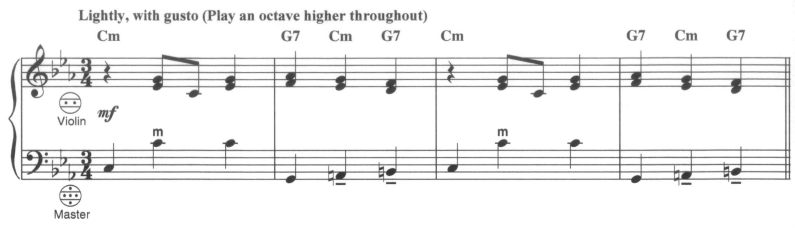

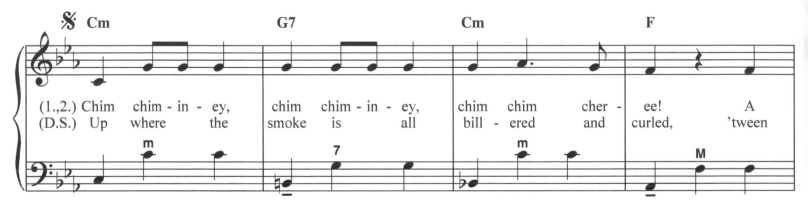

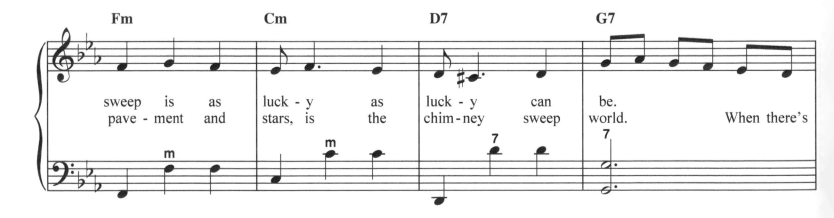

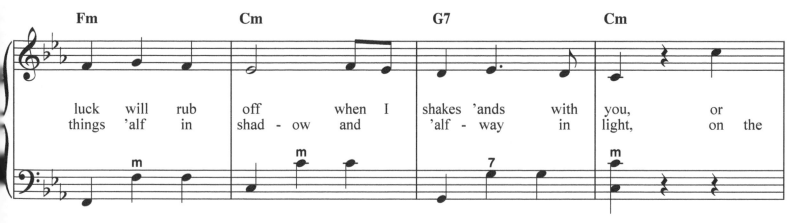

luck will rub off when I shakes 'ands with you, or
things 'alf in shad - ow and 'alf - way in light, on the

To Coda ⊕

blow me a kiss and that's luck - y too.
roof - tops of Lon - don, coo, what a

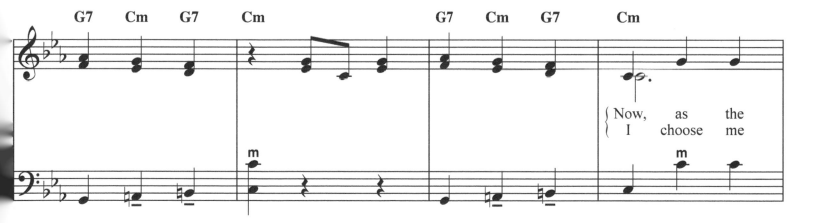

Now, as the
I choose me

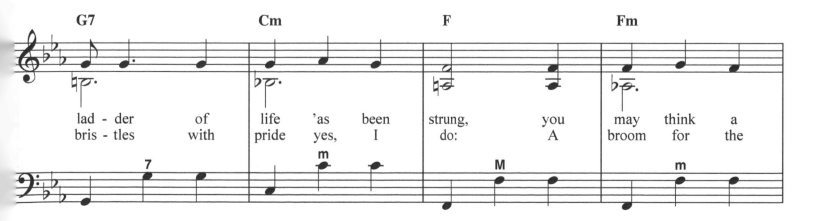

lad - der of life 'as been strung, you may think a
bris - tles with pride yes, I do: A broom for the

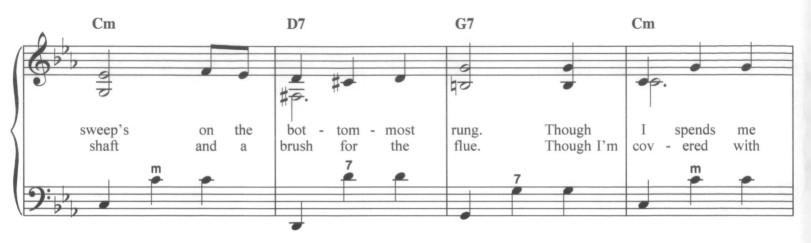

sweep's   on   the   bot - tom - most   rung.   Though   I   spends   me
shaft   and   a   brush   for   the   flue.   Though I'm   cov - ered   with

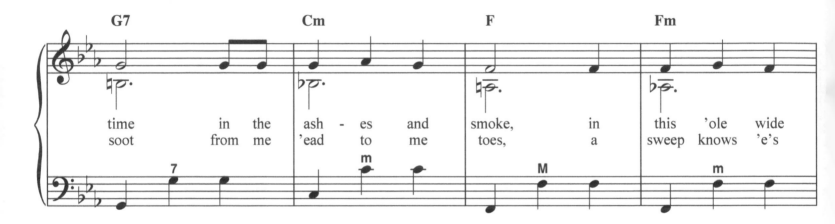

time   in   the   ash - es   and   smoke,   in   this   'ole   wide
soot   from   me   'ead   to   me   toes,   a   sweep   knows   'e's

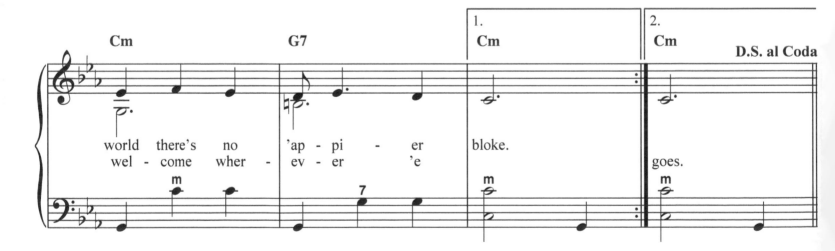

world   there's   no   'ap - pi -   er   bloke.
wel - come   wher -   ev - er   'e   goes.

D.S. al Coda

CODA

sight.   Chim   chim - in - ey,   chim   chim - in - ey,

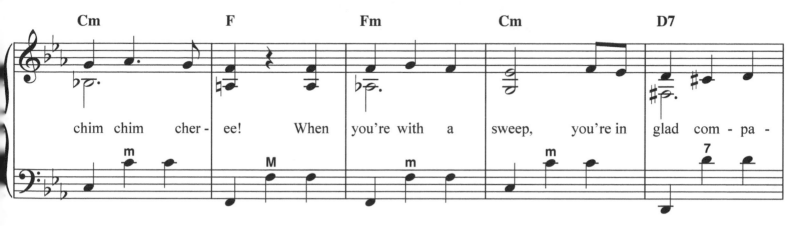

chim chim cher - ee! When you're with a sweep, you're in glad com - pa -

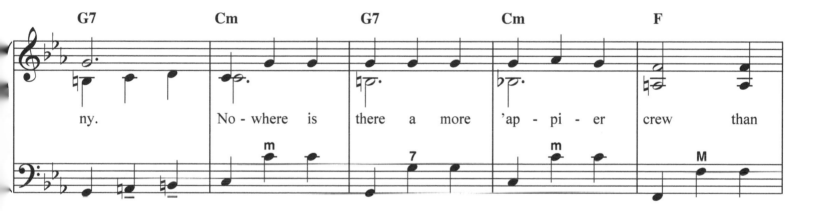

ny. No - where is there a more 'ap - pi - er crew than

them wot sings "Chim chim cher - ee, chim cher - oo!"

Chim chim - in - ey, chim chim cher - ee, chim cher - oo!

IT'S A SMALL WORLD

from Disneyland Resort® and Magic Kingdom® Park

Words and Music by RICHARD M. SHERMAN
and ROBERT B. SHERMAN

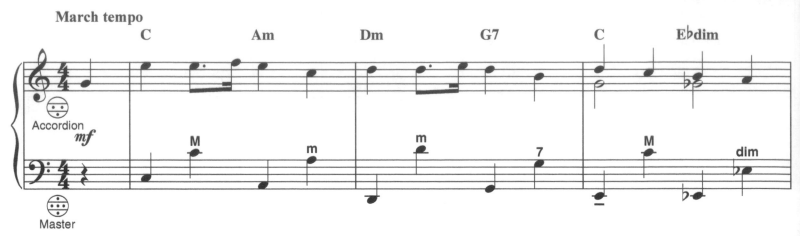

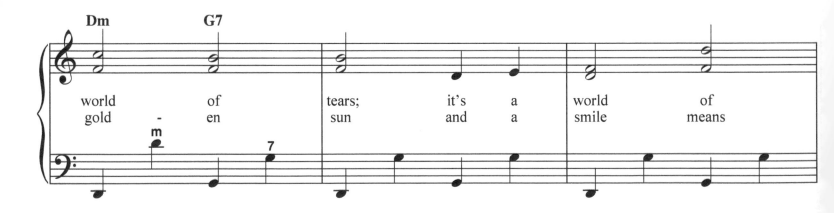

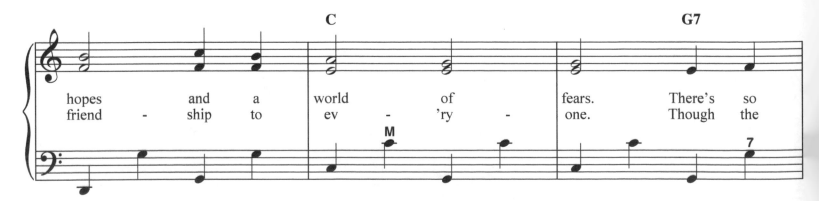

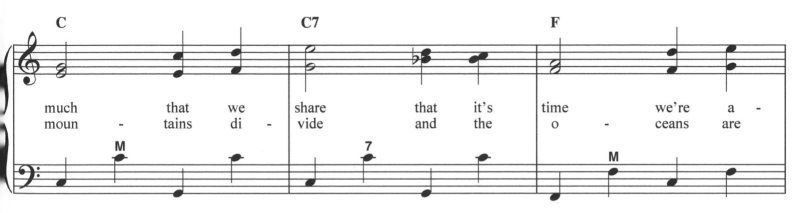

much — that we share that it's time we're a -
moun - tains di - vide that and the o - ceans are

ware it's a small world af - ter
wide, it's a small world world af - ter

all.
all. It's a

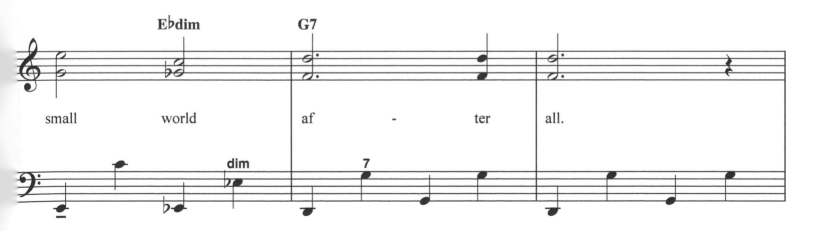

small world af - ter all.

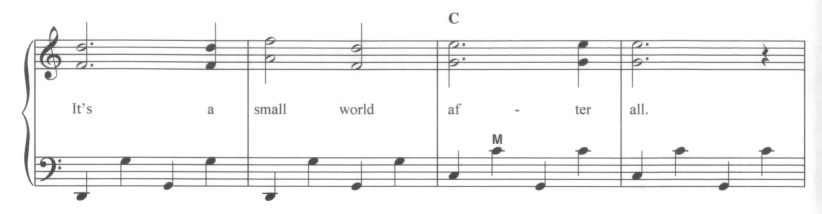

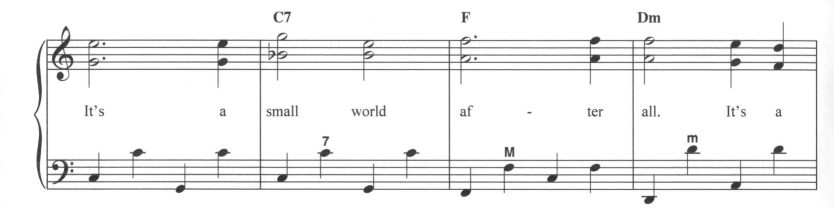

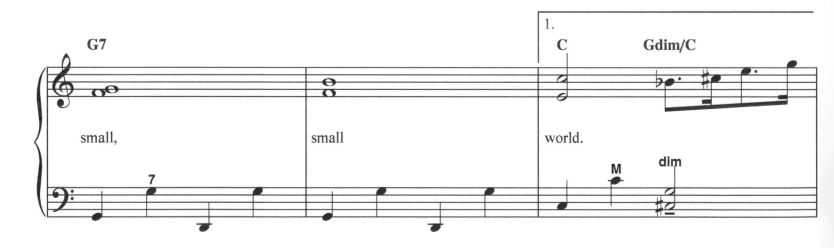

YOU'LL BE IN MY HEART
(Pop Version)
from Walt Disney Pictures' TARZAN™

Words and Music by
PHIL COLLINS

*Bass notes

cry.

C

%F

For one so small, you seem so strong. ___
Why can't they un-der-stand the way we feel? ___

C/F **F**

My arms will hold you, keep you safe and warm. ___
They just don't trust ___ what they can't ex - plain. ___

C/F **F**

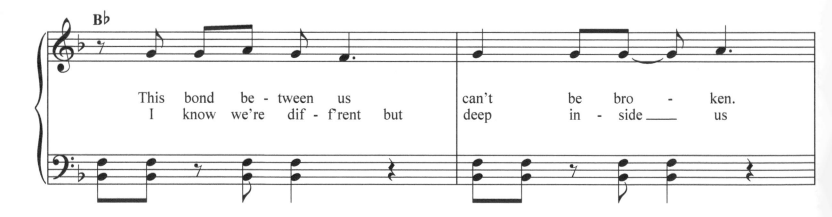

Bb

This bond be - tween us can't be bro - ken.
I know we're dif - f'rent but deep in - side ___ us

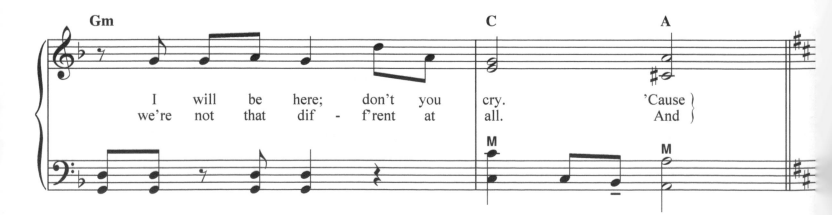

Gm

I will be here; don't you cry.
we're not that dif - f'rent at all.

C **A**

'Cause }
And }

M **M**

you'll be in my heart, yes, you'll be in my

heart from this day on, ___ now and for - ev - er -

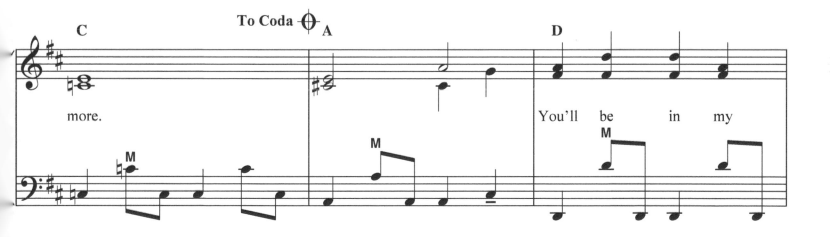

more. You'll be in my

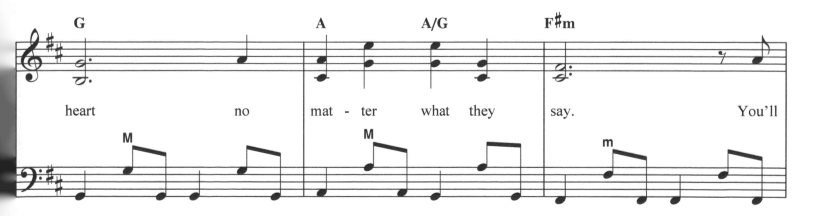

heart no mat - ter what they say. You'll

be here in ____ my heart al - ways.

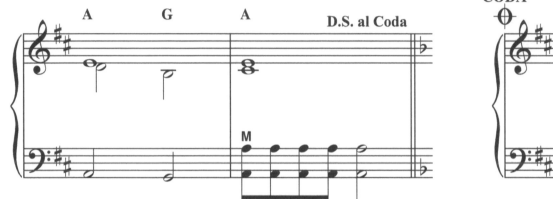

D.S. al Coda

CODA

Don't

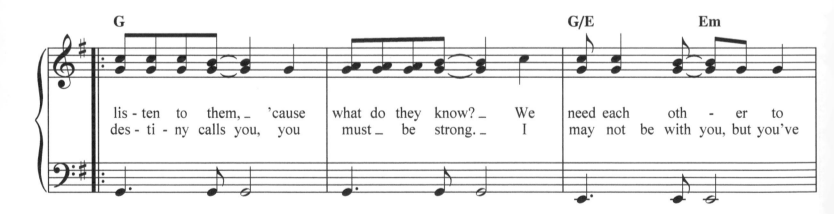

lis - ten to them, _ 'cause what do they know? _ We need each oth - er to
des - ti - ny calls you, you must _ be strong. _ I may not be with you, but you've

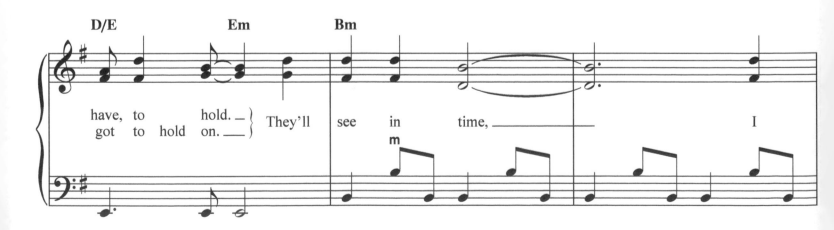

have, to hold. _ } They'll see in time, _____ I
got to hold on. _ }

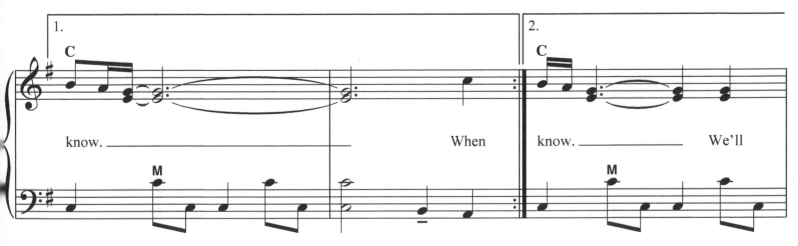

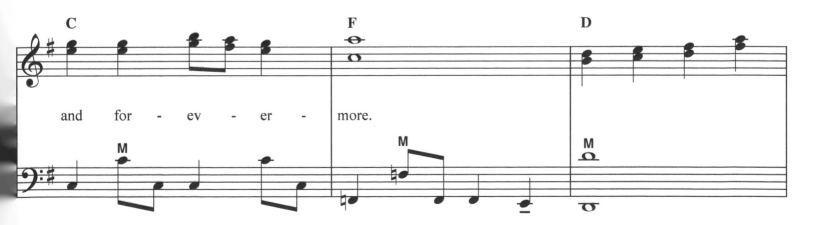

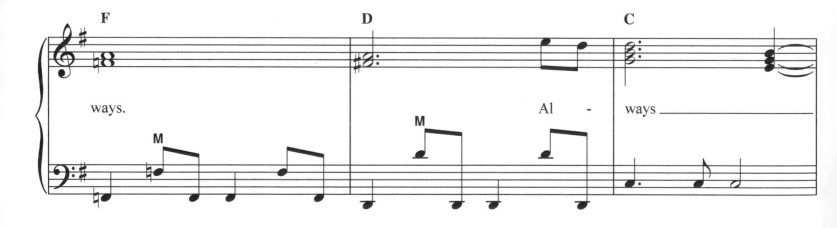

there for you al-ways, al-ways and al - ways. __

Just look o - ver your shoul-der. Just look

o - ver your shoul-der. Just look o - ver your shoul-der;

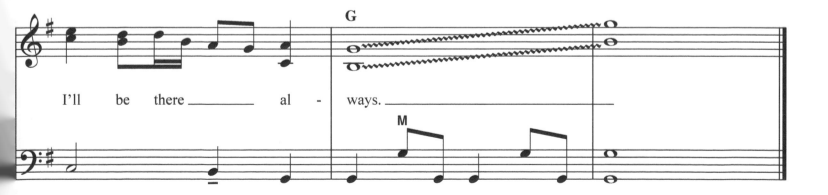

I'll be there _____ al - ways. _____

LET IT GO
from Disney's Animated Feature FROZEN

Music and Lyrics by KRISTEN ANDERSON-LOPEZ
and ROBERT LOPEZ

The snow glows white on the moun-tain to-night; _ not a

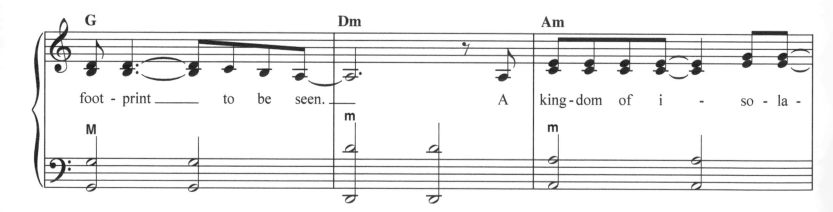

foot-print _____ to be seen. ___ A king-dom of i - so - la -

- tion, and it looks like I'm the queen.

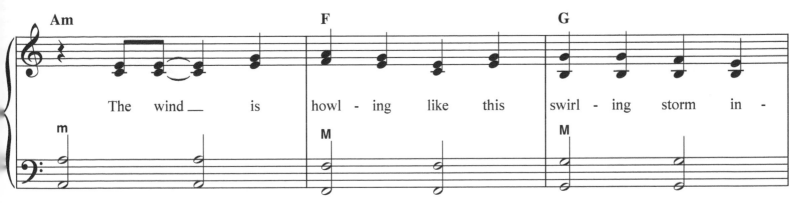

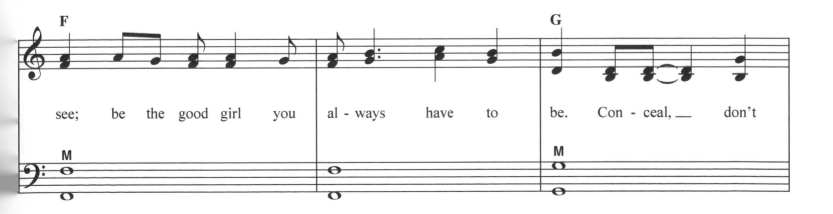

40

feel, don't let them know... Well, now

they know. Let it go, let it go;
let it go;

can't hold it back any-more. Let it go,
I am one with the wind and sky. Let it go,

let it go; turn a-way and slam the
let it go; you'll nev - er see me

door. ___
cry. ___
I don't ___ care ___ what they're
Here I ___ stand, ___ and

To Coda ⊕

going to ___ say; ___ let the storm rage ___ on. ___ The
here I'll ___ stay; ___ let the storm rage ___ on. ___

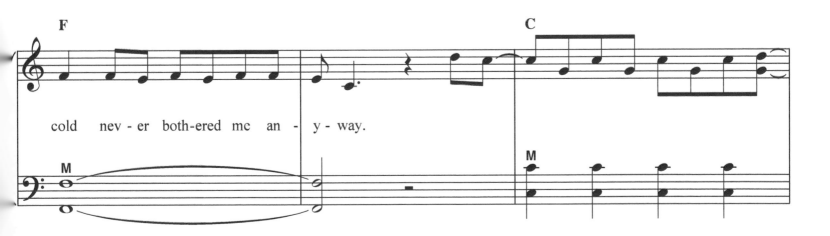

cold nev - er both-ered me an - y - way.

It's fun - ny how some dis - tance makes

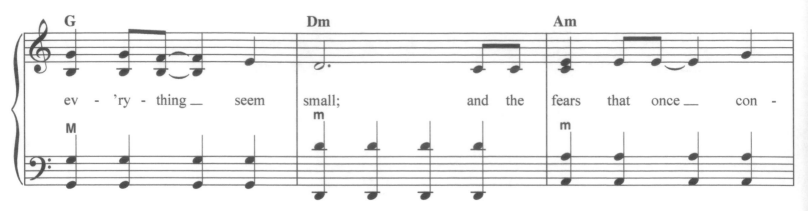

ev - 'ry - thing __ seem small; and the fears that once __ con -

trolled me can't get to me __ at all. It's time __ to

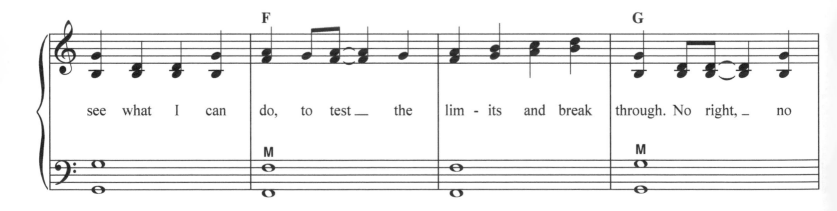

see what I can do, to test __ the lim - its and break through. No right, __ no

D.S. al Coda

wrong, no rules for me. __ I'm free! Let it go, __

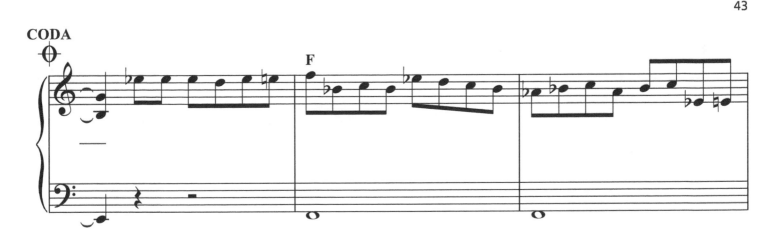

all a - round.＿　　　And one＿ thought crys - tal - liz - es

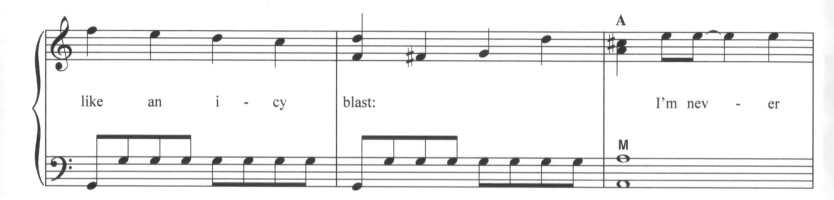

like an i - cy blast:　　　I'm nev - er

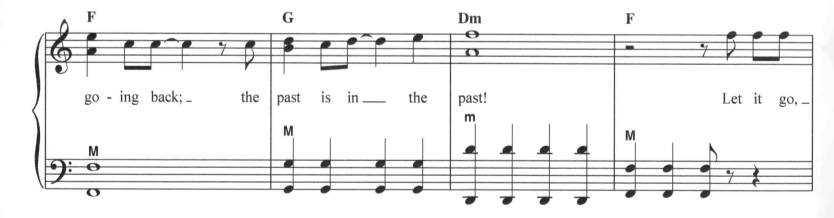

go - ing back;＿ the past is in＿ the past!　　Let it go,＿

＿ let it go,＿　　and I'll rise＿ like the break＿ of

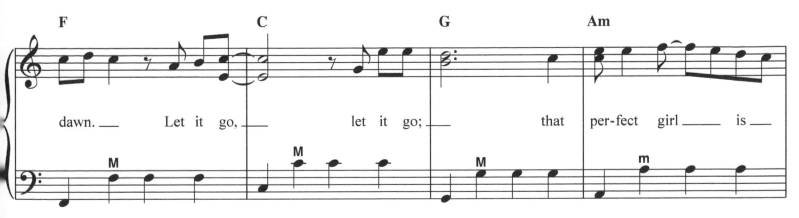

dawn.___ Let it go,___ let it go;___ that per-fect girl___ is___

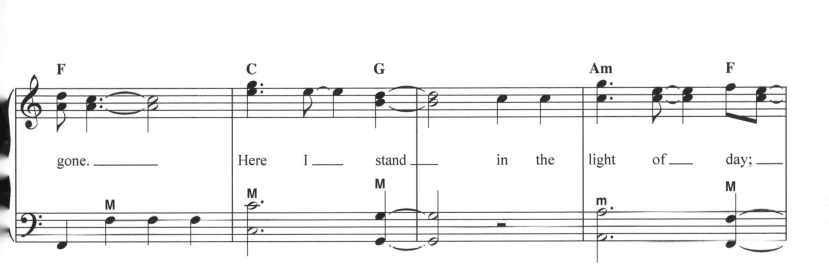

gone._____ Here I___ stand___ in the light of___ day;___

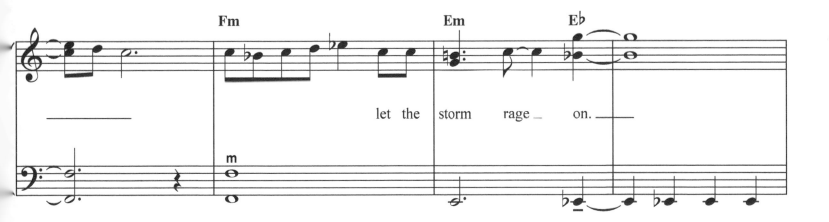

___ let the storm rage___ on.___

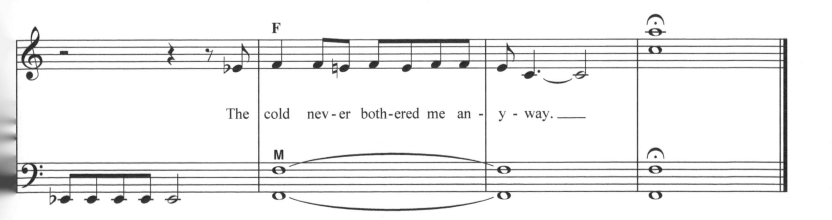

The cold nev-er both-ered me an-y-way.___

UNDER THE SEA
from Walt Disney's THE LITTLE MERMAID

Music by ALAN MENKEN
Lyrics by HOWARD ASHMAN

Just look __ at the world a - round you,
But fish __ in the bowl is luck - y,

right here __ on the
they in ___ for a

o - cean floor.
wors - er fate.

Such won - der - ful things sur - round you.
One day __ when the boss get hun - gry

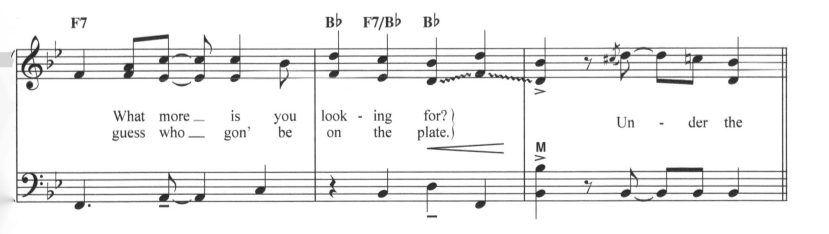

What more __ is you
guess who __ gon' be

look - ing for?
on the plate.

Un - der the

sea,

un - der the sea.

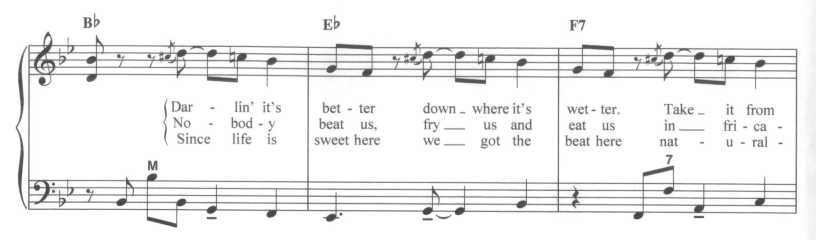

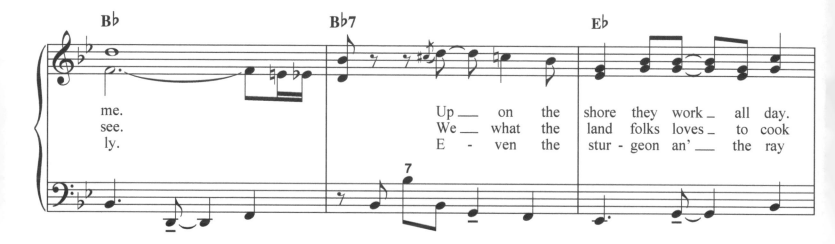

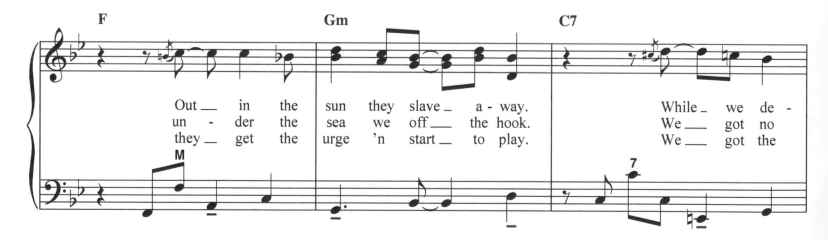

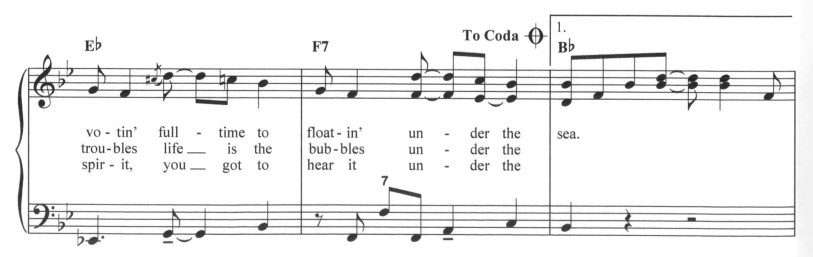

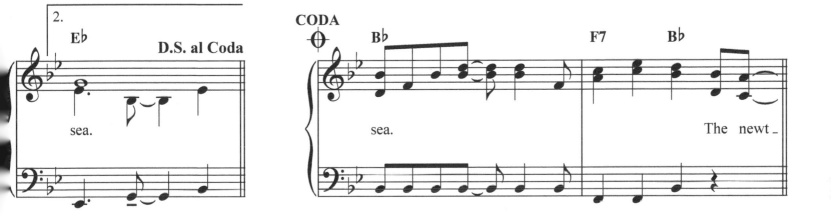

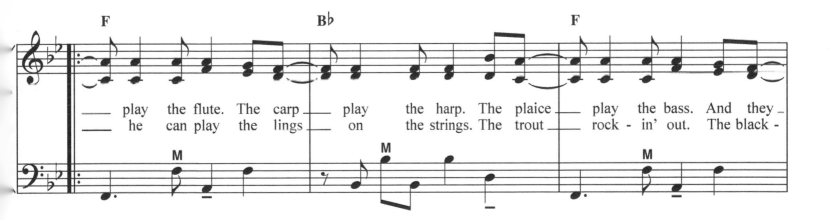

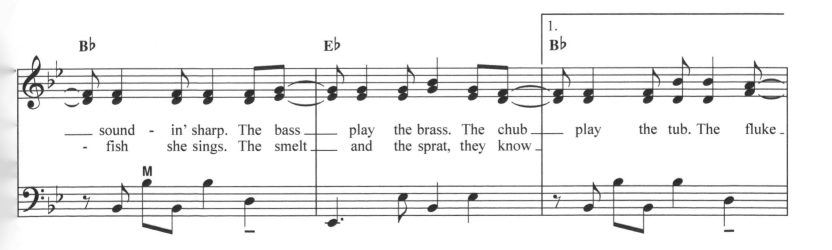

is the Duke of Soul. The ray ___ ___ where it's at. An'

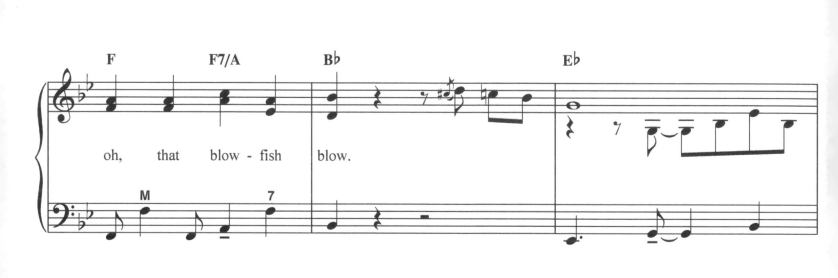

oh, that blow - fish blow.

Un-der the

sea. Un — der the sea.

When the sar - dine be - gin___ the be - guine it's mu - sic to

me.   What _ do they   got? A lot ___ of sand.

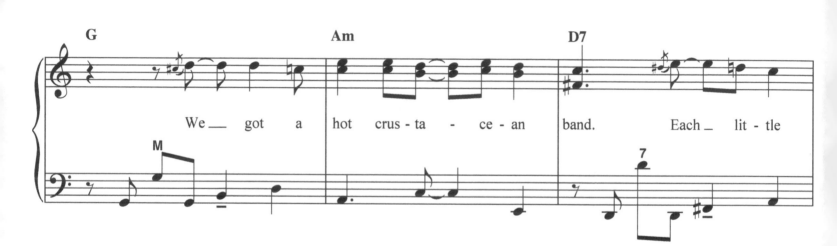

We _ got a   hot crus - ta - ce - an   band.   Each _ lit - tle

clam here   know _ how to jam ___ here   un - der the   sea.

Each lit - tle   slug here cut - tin' a   rug here   un - der the

53

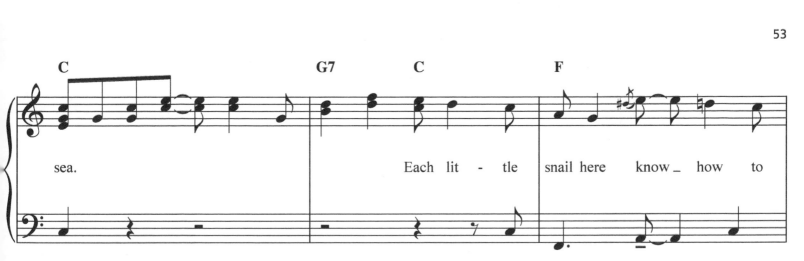

sea.   Each lit - tle   snail here   know _   how   to

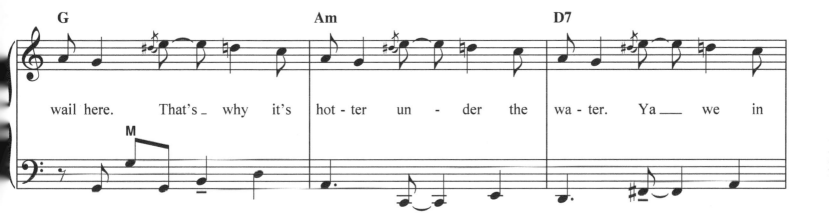

wail here.   That's _ why   it's   hot - ter   un - der   the   wa - ter.   Ya ___   we   in

luck here   down _   in   the   muck here   un - der   the   sea.

A WHOLE NEW WORLD
from Walt Disney's ALADDIN

Music by ALAN MENKEN
Lyrics by TIM RICE

This arrangement may be played by a solo accordion, two accordions or an accordion band. The left hand may be played by Accordion 1 and Accordion 2.

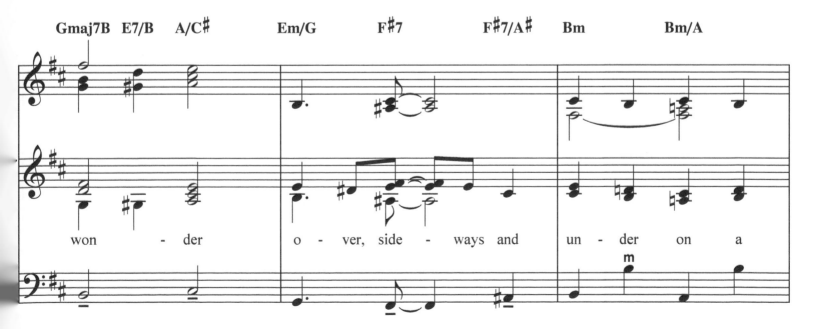

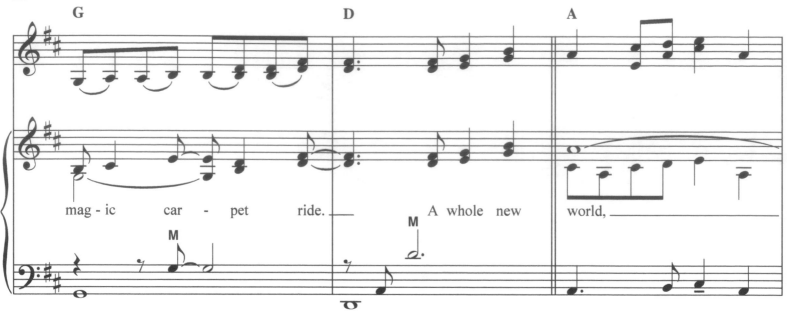

mag - ic car - pet ride. ____ A whole new world, ____

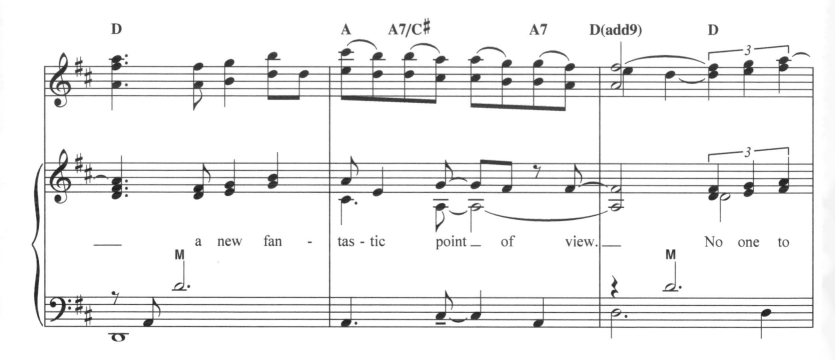

___ a new fan - tas - tic point _ of view. __ No one to

tell us no or where to go or say we're on - ly dream -

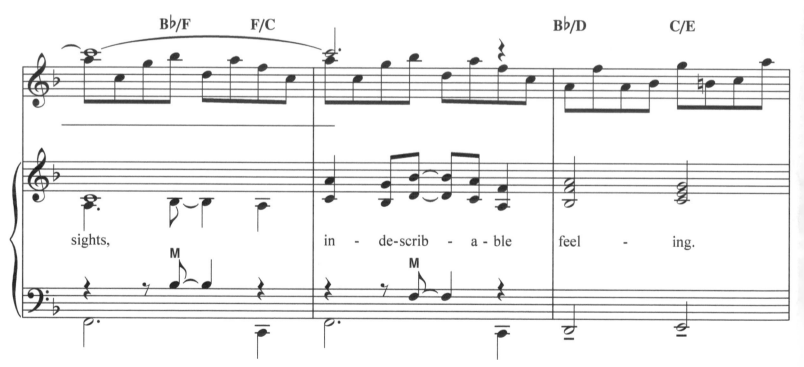

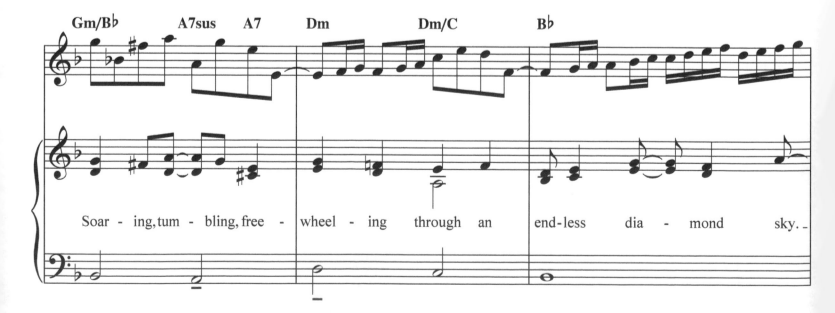

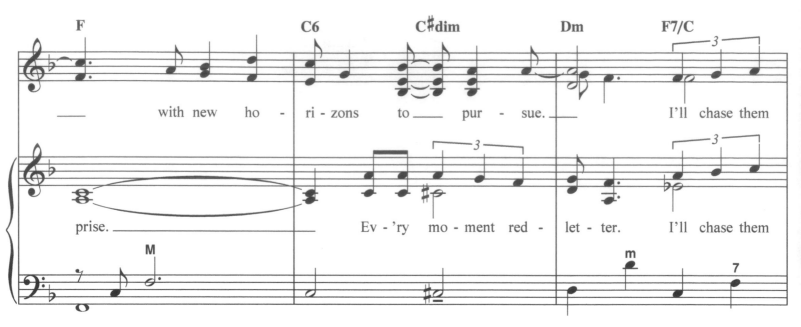

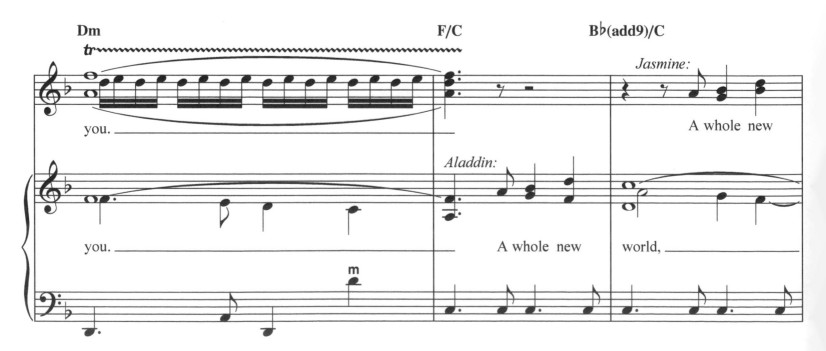

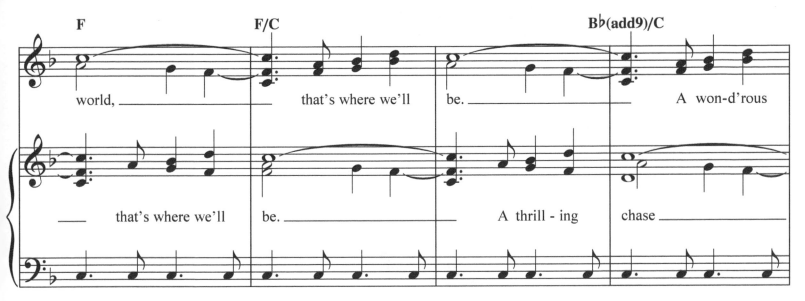

world, _____ that's where we'll be. _____ A won-d'rous

that's where we'll be. _____ A thrill - ing chase _____

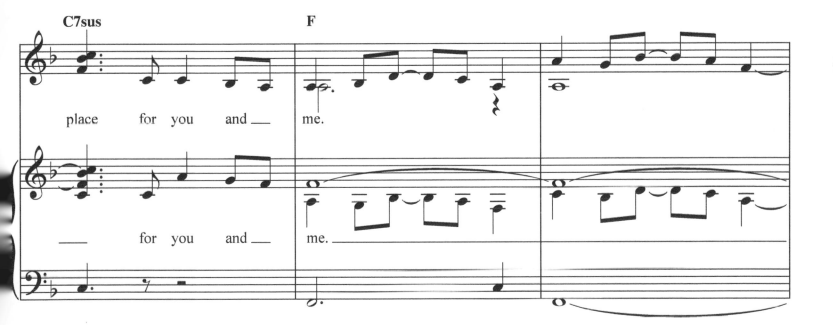

place for you and __ me.

__ for you and __ me. _____

ZIP-A-DEE-DOO-DAH
from Walt Disney's SONG OF THE SOUTH

Words by RAY GILBERT
Music by ALLIE WRUBEL

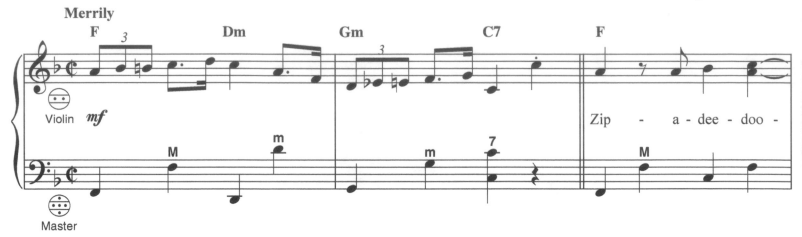

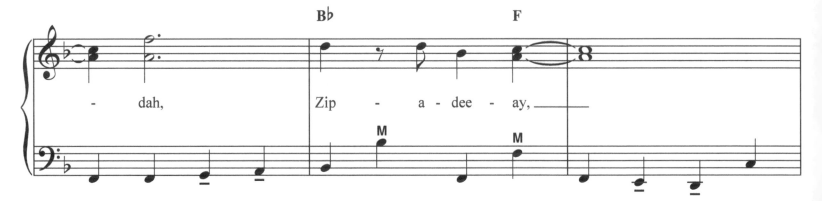

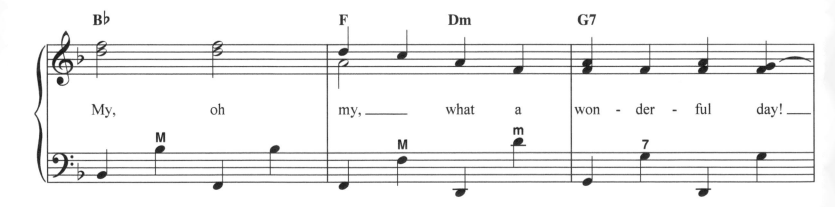

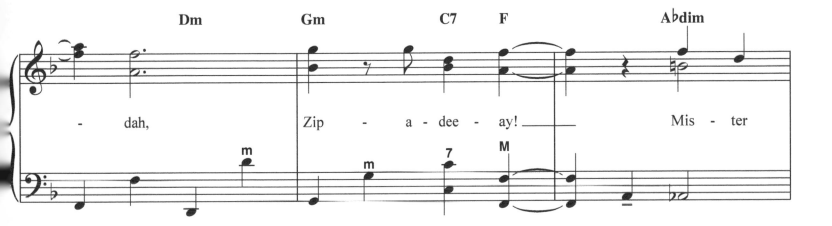

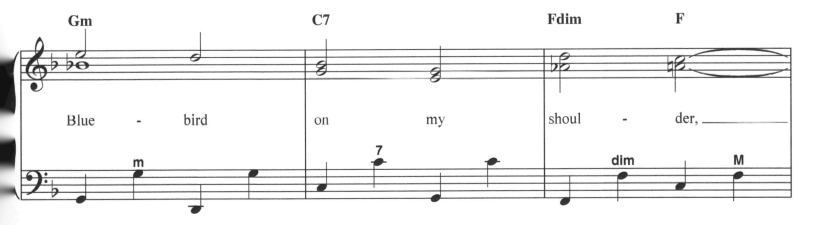

Ev - 'ry - thing is "sat - is - fact - ch'll." Zip - a - dee - doo -

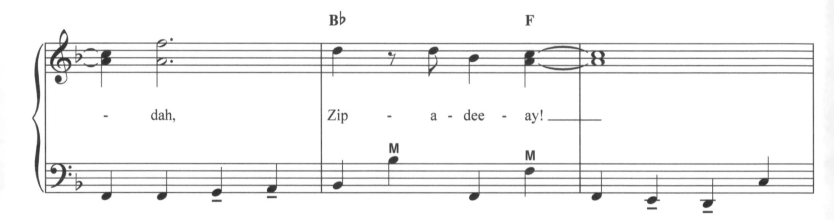

- dah, Zip - a - dee - ay! _____

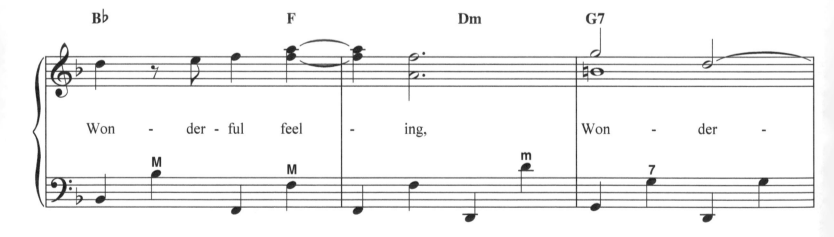

Won - der - ful feel - ing, Won - der -

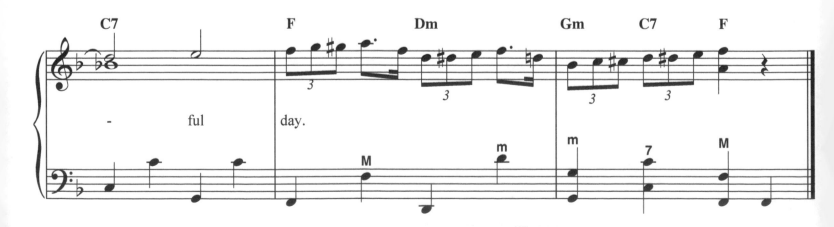

- ful day.